Virtuous Women of Valor

Discover the Grace and Wisdom to be the
Military Wife God Desires You to be

Ester Johnson

Ester Johnson
II Cor 1:3-4

PRESS

Virtuous Women of Valor
Discover the Grace and Wisdom to be the Military Wife God
Desires You to be
by Ester Johnson

Printed in the United States of America

ISBN 9781609577766

www.xulonpress.com

Dedication

I dedicate this book to those who have gone before me, kept the faith, and discipled me in how to be the best military wife I can be to my husband.

I also dedicate this book to my husband and my best friend, Rob, who has not only supported my endeavors for years but has also been my biggest encourager and helper through the joys and trials of life.

A special thanks to my editor, Jean Pennington, who graciously edited this book.

Table of Contents

Introduction

My desire in writing this devotional is to encourage military wives to seek out Scripture for biblical answers to common military challenges. My hope is that you will dive into Scripture and look at the good, the questionable, and the bad choices of women in the Bible who have gone before us and lived out their lives for us to view and learn from. Being married to someone whose primary mission in life is to serve our country is difficult at best. Yet, Scripture is filled with the wisdom we need in order to please God while serving our husbands. I hope you can gain further insight into your own soul and develop a deeper relationship with the Lord.

I recommend using the book as a personal devotional guide and thereby allow God's Word to speak to your life. If you should use it in a group setting, first read and study each chapter, before meeting as a group to discuss the practical ways you can apply biblical truths to your lives.

While this book is primarily targeted to the military wife, anyone with a family member in the military may benefit from the devotional, as will women whose husbands travel frequently. Some might find this to be a perfect gift for a woman in a serious relationship with a military member or for a newlywed who has not yet faced the hardships that come with being married to a man in the military. I hope this book will find its way into the hands of all who can use it to grow closer to the Lord.

"Blessed *be* God, even the Father of our Lord Jesus Christ, the Father of mercies, and the God of all comfort; Who comforteth us in all our tribulation, that we may be able to comfort them which are in any trouble, by the comfort wherewith we ourselves are comforted of God." 2 Corinthians 1:3-4.

Chapter 1

Ahhh, Love

Dear Diary,

I've seen many people come through our home lately and there doesn't seem to be any real privacy. Daddy, who proudly retired as a Marine Corps Brigadier General, makes sure that he knows everything that is going on with the family, including my love life. For some reason, I get the sense that he feels threatened by all the young men who thrive off the same adventure that he once pursued. Now that he is well-off and settled, he doesn't want to see any of his hard work given over to anyone other than his own son or family.

Anyway, I get to meet the different men that come by to visit Daddy. My brother Sam often joins in on the conversation if he's home. He's a Marine, too. I love listening to their different war stories and I am more than happy to chat with them when I can. One of the men that frequently stops by to see Daddy and Sam is a Marine named Marc. You would think that he and Sam were brothers by the way they carry on together. Over the past few years I've watched them laugh until they cry, listened to them passionately sing hymns, observed them lend a willing hand at church, and overall serve God wholeheartedly. Marc sings with such tenderness and worshipfulness to God. He is BY FAR the handsomest man I have ever seen. I find myself dreaming about him constantly.

Sam and Marc joined the Marines together (infantry, no less) and treat their service as a "rite of passage". They've been able to get assigned to the same battalion and are constantly pushing each other to be the absolute best they can be. I worried and prayed for them more times than I can count when they were in combat during the past several years. But that turmoil all melts away when they return home as heroes! I remember their last homecoming: the sunlight dancing off the "Welcome Home" balloons and banners as the company stood perfectly still (and completely attractive) in formation while the loved ones and well-wishers watched in eager anticipation. The Commanding Officer recounted all the great things the men had accomplished during the deployment, but truth be told, we couldn't wait for him to stop talking! Once he finished and dismissed the unit, I ran up to and hugged Sam and Marc out of relief and pride. Yet, after both deployments they've come back different somehow - changed by war: stronger, bolder, more passionate about everything, and even a little distant.

Daddy has been trying to get Marc to marry my older sister. I'm glad he thinks Marc is "worthy" of our family, but I don't think he understands that he is hurting me. Deep down I believe it's all about his agenda to keep an eye on Marc. Marc is young and vibrant and the people around here really look up to him. Plus, he's considered a war hero and genuine leader by his Marines. In fact, the local newspaper did a story on how similar Marc and Daddy are in their accomplishments. I just don't think I can handle it if he marries my sister. I can't believe Daddy hasn't picked up on my hints about Marc and me. But I need to be careful about what I say, because my sister and I are going to be paired up with whomever Daddy thinks we should marry. His VERY old-fashioned ideals and traditions are burdensome and often annoying to me. I guess this whole situation wouldn't be so bad except I have already started to fall in love. . .

Dear Diary,

Daddy did it! I can't believe that Daddy did it. I'm devastated. My heart is genuinely torn in two. Daddy asked Marc how he would feel about marrying my older sister. How could he?

Dear Diary,

Now what? Marc refuses to marry my sister because he doesn't think he's good enough for the family. Don't get me wrong. I'm very thankful he won't marry her. So I guess she'll be getting married to someone else that Daddy loves. The hard thing about it all is that Marc's response tells me that I have absolutely no hope of marrying him. I've been crying for days. I even think Marc's noticed how upset I've been. Why does Daddy have to be so difficult and heartless! Ohhhh, my life is over!

Dear Diary,

Marc just proposed to me! He told me that he and Daddy met earlier today and that Daddy agreed to allow him to marry ME! Can this be real? My heart is going through a roller coaster of emotions right now because after Marc asked me to marry him and gave me my beautiful ring, he quietly told me that he is returning to Afghanistan as an Individual Augmentee for a seven month deployment. Oh, I hope Marc doesn't get himself killed! He said that he volunteered as an IA so that he could save up money for our upcoming life together and show Daddy that he is worthy of me. I'm praying so vigilantly for him. Does Marc really love me that much? I'm just in agony to see him again. This is all so bittersweet. Please, God, bring him back safely to me and help these months to fly!

Dear Diary,

I am soon to be married to my Love. He's finally returned from this exasperatingly long deployment. Oh, he looked so striking when we all greeted him at the airport. He was still a mite dirty and his uniform seemed a little bare, but he looked so dashing. He's mine! He's really going to be mine forever. Daddy won't go back on his word now because he'd look like a fool. I'm going to marry *my* Marc! Sam is thrilled, too. Now he and Marc are really going to be brothers.

Dear Diary,

Our wedding is one week away! I wonder what it will be like to kiss my husband and to gaze into his green eyes as his bride

Haven't we all been there? Nearly every woman can remember the exact details about how she first met and fell in love with her husband. I can still picture my husband the very first time that I saw him. Some of you may not remember the first time you saw your husbands but you can probably remember the first time you "saw" him as someone different – special.

Michal, the daughter of King Saul, was a woman who fell in love with her brother's best friend and was actually able to marry him. Let's look at the first stage of their love and make some practical applications for ourselves.

The Biblical Background

God miraculously delivered the Israelites from their slavery to the Egyptians through the leadership of Moses in roughly 1448 B.C. After receiving the Ten Commandments and the rest of the Law on Mount Sinai, the people wandered in the wilderness for forty years because of their lack of faith in God (Numbers 13:17-33). In fact, even Moses did not enter into what we now know as the country of Israel. Instead, God raised up Joshua, Moses' right hand man, to lead the Jews to conquer the land promised to Abraham and his descendants. As the new generation obeyed God much of the land was conquered, but as time passed by, the Israelites disobeyed God by intermarrying with the natives of the land. As a result, the Jews' hearts wandered from God as they began practicing a form of syncretism (mixing worship of the one true God with that of the local deities). In fact things got so bad that, "every man did what was right in his own eyes." God gave them over to their enemies. But when they cried out to Him for help, He raised up judges (like Samson and Gideon) to rule over His people. This pattern then played out in the nation's history for about 300 years: 1. God would raise up a judge to deliver the people from their neighbors and their sin, 2. the people would repent and obey for a short period of time and prosper, 3. they would then become complacent and go back to their old way of living, 4. God would discipline the Israelites for their sin, by allowing them to be taken captive by the neighbor peoples until they cried out to God for help. This cycle finally came to head under the judge and prophet Samuel. The people had grown tired of judges, and wanted to have a king like the nations around them. So God told Samuel to appoint Saul as the first king in the history of Israel. Consequently, Saul ruled the nation from approximately 1050 - 1010 B.C. While Saul's life started with strong convictions and an obedient heart, his latter years were marked by repeated sin and subsequent disillusionment as God's blessing was removed from his life and then placed upon David. Michal, Saul's daughter, and her brother Jonathan were eyewitnesses to their father's triumphs and tragedies.

Meditation Passage: Psalm 112

Focal Passage: 1 Samuel 17 - 18

1. Read Psalm 112 and note the qualities of a godly man. Then compare these qualities with what you know of David (see 1 Sam. 18 for a good summary of his character). What are the qualities that you see in David that make him a man worthy of desire?_____

_____
_____
_____
_____
_____
_____
_____

2. Again reflecting on Psalm 112, what are the qualities in your spouse that make him worthy to be desired? _____

_____
_____
_____
_____

• As you consider your husband in light of Psalm 112, how can you specifically pray for and assist him in growing in godliness? _____

_____
_____
_____

3. Read 1 Samuel 18:1-5. What opportunities do you think Michal might have had to get to know David because of his friendship with Jonathan? _____
_____
_____
_____
_____
_____
_____
_____

4. Notice that Michal is said to "love" David several times in 1 Samuel 18:20-29. Our English word "love" translates a Hebrew word that has a relatively wide spectrum of nuanced meanings. It may describe the relationship between God and man (Psalm 146:8; 2 Samuel 12:24), the closeness shared between a man and woman involved in a sexual relationship (Genesis 24:67; 1 Kings 11:1; 2 Samuel 13:15), a person's affection for a family member or close friend (Genesis 22:2), a high respect for some ideal or character trait (Proverbs 12:1; Micah 6:8), or even a desire for a certain type of food (Genesis 27:9). What conclusions regarding Michal's love for David that you might be able to draw from this short word study?
_____
_____
_____

5. For good or bad, have you or anyone you have known "fallen for" the man in the uniform instead of truly loving the man himself?
_____

- While many women today spend a great deal of time and energy focusing on the wedding ceremony, the reality is that the eager bride-to-be must look beyond the wedding day and learn as much as possible about her future husband before the big day comes on the calendar.

• No matter how hard you try, you will not know your husband completely the moment you exchange your vows. In fact, you will find some things about him that are difficult or troublesome before and after your wedding ceremony. However, this does not give you good cause to resent him or keep a mental list of his shortcomings to hold against him at a later time. Instead, as you commit your marriage and your husband to God, He can give you the grace to rise above the trials caused by your husband's sinful weaknesses. You must learn to turn to God to have your needs met. This will free you to love your husband unconditionally, even if you end up being in a bad situation. Read 2 Corinthians 12:9-10 and summarize how you can apply its lessons to your marriage. Why was Paul able to "glory" in his trials? How can you relate this passage to difficulties you experience in marriage?_____

_____
_____
_____
_____
_____
_____

6. Read 1 Samuel 18:7, 13-16, 23-30; 19:8; 22:1-2; 23:1-5 and note David's military responsibilities._____

_____
_____
_____
_____

• What are the military responsibilities of your spouse?_____

_____
_____

- In what ways do you ever make it difficult for your spouse to carry out his commitment to the military? How does your negative attitude and complaining spirit affect him? Read Philippians 2:14-15 and 1 Thessalonians 5:16-18. If you are completely trusting in God, what will your attitude be when troubles come? _____

  _____

  _____

  _____

  _____

  _____

- David was highly honored in both the Israelite military and kingdom. No matter how trivial or significant a position you think your spouse has in his particular branch of service, you can encourage him to give all glory to the Lord even when he finds himself in a difficult circumstance. Your response to his situation will either help or hinder him in his relationship with God. Focusing on Colossians 3:22-4:1, what should your spouse's attitude be to his authority, regardless of where he lines up in the military hierarchy?_____

  _____

  _____

  _____

  _____

  _____

  _____

- What were David's responses to his position and the commands from his leader as found in 1 Samuel 18:5, 13, 14, 18, 23, 27, 28? _____

  _____

  _____

  _____

7. 1 Samuel 18:20 says that Michal loved David. What emotions do you think Michal went through based on what happened in 1 Samuel 18:18-19? _____

_____

_____

_____

- How have you suffered disappointment involving your spouse or your relationship? What differing emotions have you felt in regards to him? Reflect on the command the Lord gives older women in Titus 2:3-5. The Lord understands that young women need time to learn to love their husbands and children. If you struggle in this duty, seek out an older and wiser Christian lady who can counsel, encourage, and disciple you. _____

_____

_____

_____

_____

_____

_____

- Have may you have caused disappointment for your spouse? What can you do to help prevent this from happening again? Read 1 Corinthians 7:10-16 and list the Biblical commands the Lord gives that apply to marital conflict. _____

_____

_____

_____

_____

_____

_____

8. Consider Saul's relationship with his daughters in 1 Samuel 18 and then read Colossians 3:21. Do you think Michal and Merab were close to each other and to their father? While the culture of their time was much more patriarchal in nature than the one we live in today,

the passage still gives us hints about how Saul viewed his daughters, which undoubtedly affected his relationship with them. _____

- Do you have a strong family support system? If not, you are not alone. You can look to the Lord as your family and reach out to the military community to develop new relationships. Genesis 2:24 gives instructions on the marriage partnership. List how you can lean upon your new friends without violating Genesis 2:24. _____

  _____

  _____

  _____

  _____

  _____

  _____

9. King Saul fought in wars, as did his son Jonathan. Is there a history of military service in your family or your husband's family?

- If you have a military legacy, how did being reared as a military family member prepare you to marry someone in the military? _____

  _____

  _____

  _____

- Reflect upon Genesis 2:23-25 and the very specific implications to marrying someone who serves in the military. Family ties can be a great support for spouses, but can also cause undue trouble for couples who face distinct challenges most civilians do not understand. Personalize Genesis 2:23-25 by putting you and your spouse's name in the verses and writing them out. _____

  _____

  _____

_____

_____

_____

_____

10. How do you think Michal felt knowing that David went to battle (1 Samuel 18:26-27) in order to pay for her dowry? This was a costly dowry that Saul was using to try to ensnare David to kill him in battle. _____

_____

_____

- How did your spouse "pay for your dowry?" For example, did he write letters, poems, buy flowers, buy jewelry, etc.

  _____

  _____

  _____

  _____

  _____

  _____

- Recall how you met your husband. Write a brief summary of how you met and how he wooed you. How did you encourage him in return?_____

  _____

  _____

  _____

  _____

  _____

  _____

11. Write your husband a letter reminding him of your first moments together as a couple.

12. What are practical ways that you can keep love fresh and youthful in light of 1 Corinthians 13? _____

_____

Chapter 2

Love Already Waning?

Dear Diary,

Ithought marriage was supposed to be so awesome. I mean, don't get me wrong, it is. Well, sort of. I'm disappointed with all the times Jeff has to go away. We've only been married for a few months. And my family won't get off my back about Jeff (they are just mad about our whirlwind romance). I am totally sick of it all! Gotta go . . . never get a break anymore (explain a little bit further why not). . .

Dear Diary,

I never thought Jeff's life would be in *real* danger. I guess I knew it in the back of my mind, but I can't even tell people what my husband *really* does.

Jeff came home today. I had made a nice dinner and put on an extra special dress. He didn't notice. Because it was so late, he ate and then went straight to bed. I cried and yelled and made quite the scene. I did NOT marry the military. I married HIM! He said I was being unreasonable, that he was sorry, that...blah, blah, blah.

Dear Diary,

Jeff confided in me today that he may have to leave home in order to protect me. Apparently he is doing some secretive work that could actually bring danger to me if he stays here much longer. I'm upset, but there is a sense of excitement too. He's totally lavished me with passion as if he won't see me again, so it is really nice. Maybe the intensity of this all will help us in the long run. I'll miss him, but maybe I can go back home and visit with family while he's gone. Why not?! I know dad doesn't really like Jeff (just because we got married so quickly) but I doubt it would bring too much trouble if I left and went there. It would be safer, too. Jeff and I could save money. Maybe Jeff would even get out of the military and come live back at home again when he's done. Hmmmm. I think I like this idea and may wait until Jeff is gone to really push it with my family.

Dear Diary,

Jeff's been gone for a really long time now. I don't hear from him, I'm lonely, and my family thinks I should just get out of the marriage while I can. They have a point. It's like I'm living as a single girl but with a ring on my left hand. More like ball and chain. It's binding and frustrating. I thought Jeff loved me but *apparently* he loves the military more than me. I've also noticed some of the guys where I go work out, and it's nice getting some attention in return! ~~They ignite a spark in me that I haven't had in awhile, and frankly, I like it.~~ NO! No, this is wrong. I am just angry. If only Jeff would try to show me he really loved me and not the military.

"Married widows" is a good name for military women whose husbands are gone frequently. You seem to be married in name only except for a few days here and there. Many times women just give up because they are too frustrated with the pull on their husbands from the government. Young marriages often collapse under the pressure of separations that occur soon after the couple marries. This strain, often paired with a lack of life experience as well as a lingering dating mindset, allows temptation to seep in quickly. Let's look at the bitterness that can build up in a marriage relationship if we aren't careful in guarding our hearts.

The Biblical Background

In Genesis 2:23-25 God established the precedent that marriage was between one man and one woman. Throughout the Old

Testament, however, we see key godly leaders involved in polygamy: Abraham, Jacob, David, Solomon, etc. These men rationalized that having multiple wives and concubines would increase the size of their families and their standing in society. Yet, Scripture bears witness to the fact that these relationships had serious downfalls. God warns in Deuteronomy 17:17 that many wives turn the heart of the husband away from God. You can see the sad truth come to fruition with Solomon in 1 Kings 11:4. In the ancient Hebrew culture one of the wife's main responsibilities was to have children. Many children were a sign of blessing by God. For example, look at Hannah's plea to the Lord for a child in 1 Samuel 1 to gain a little bit of insight into the pain of one who was unable to bear children.

Meditation Passage: Colossians 3

Focal Passages: 1 Samuel 19; 25:44; 2 Samuel 3:12-16; 5:13; 6:12-23; 1 Chronicles 15:29

1. Michal helped David escape from her father's grasp, but then lied to him to make it sound like she was forced to aid her husband. Are there any clues from Scripture that suggest that Michal may have been caught up in the excitement of the moment and still living in the "romance period" of her and David's relationship? _____

_____

_____

_____

_____

- Have you ever lied to get yourself out of trouble (even a tiny, harmless white lie)? How did you justify your actions?

_____

_____

- Have you ever lied to help your spouse get out of duty or work? _____

_____

_____

25

- Have you noticed any negative consequences to the lies you mentioned in the previous bullets? Did anything good come from your deception, even short-term? _____
  _____
  _____
  _____
  _____

2. Read Exodus 20:16, Jeremiah 9:5, Zechariah 8:16, and Ephesians 4:25. Is there ever a right time to lie? Whom are you ultimately trusting in, when you deceive or lie to someone?_____
_____
_____

- Please note: While the Bible records godly men and women being deceitful, it nowhere condones their actions. Instead, the negative consequences of each individual's exploits are clearly seen as you read through their life stories. For instance, take Abram (later renamed 'Abraham' by God [Genesis 17:5]), who in Genesis 12:10-20 had to flee to Egypt when there was a famine in the land in order to provide for his household. Yet, because his wife Sarai (later renamed 'Sarah' by God [Genesis 17:15-16]) was a very beautiful woman, he feared that the pagan Egyptians would slay him in order to take her for themselves. So he devised a crafty plan, convincing her to tell the violent Egyptians that she was his sister. After all, she was his half-sister, right (see Gen. 20:12)? He wasn't technically telling a lie, was he? Yes, he was! He was deceiving the Egyptians and his actions show that he did not trust God to protect him from the dangers in which he found himself.

- Ironically, Pharaoh did take Sarai into his house, and with her came great plagues from God. Consequently, Pharaoh called out Abraham for his trickery and as a result, the 'heathen' Pharaoh appears more noble than the 'righteous' Abraham in this story. After this episode, you would think that Abraham would have learned his lesson. He did not. He repeats the very same ruse with Abimelech, the king of a city named Gerar (Gen. 20:1-18). Again, God intervened and held Abraham accountable for his lying ways. In the short term, it appears Abraham will not reap any negative consequences from his deceit, and that's how it often is with us. Yet, that's not the end of the story. Fast forward in time to Genesis 26 when Abraham is dead and his promised son Isaac is at least 75 years old. Isaac is confronted with the very same situation that Abraham was. So what does Isaac do? He calls his wife Rebekah his sister out of fear for his life (vv. 6-7)! God still blessed Isaac DESPITE his sinful lying (vv. 12-14), but the pattern of deception was firmly entrenched in this family beginning with Sarah's deception in Genesis 18:1-15. By nature we are all deceivers. These Bible characters illustrate what is true of us all.

3. Read 1 Samuel 25:44. Michal was separated from David for a long time and then given to another man. How do you think Michal felt about David after this time span? _____

_____

_____

- What are some passages that could provide comfort to someone who feels a sense of abandonment from their spouse? Look up the words "comfort", "peace", and "hope" in a concordance and read those verses. Select a few that speak to your situation and memorize them so that you may be able to recall them when the temptation arises to harbor bitterness. Who has God promised to be to you even when others abandon you? Reflect on Psalm 27:9-11.

_____

_____

_____

_____

_____

_____

- How do deployments or even long work schedules extinguish the marital spark? _____
  _____
  _____
  _____
  _____
  _____
  _____

- What are some very specific ways to keep the love flowing while you are separated from your spouse? List at least 10.

  1. Pray for your spouse! _____
  2. Write letters or emails to your spouse. _____
  3. _____
  4. _____
  5. _____
  6. _____
  7. _____
  8. _____
  9. _____
  10. _____

- List additional practical ways to avoid desiring another man while your spouse is gone.

  1. Not ever allow myself to be alone with someone of the opposite sex. _____
  2. Remember the good things about my spouse's appearance. _____
  3. _____
  4. _____
  5. _____
  6. _____
  7. _____
  8. _____

9. _____

10. _____

4. My husband and I are extremely close. While he was deployed for a year we were able to have 2 weeks of R&R after he had been away for 9 months. We had both changed in so many ways: emotionally, physically, mentally and spiritually. The excitement and anticipation would be difficult to explain, however, I just didn't know what to expect. Questions like, "Will he still find me as attractive as before; how have the war experiences he has faced changed him; how will the kids react to having Daddy home and then having to say good bye again; Will he care that the house isn't run the exact same way as before, etc?" Reuniting can be very awkward even in the best situations. Michal was returned to David under some unusual circumstances. 2 Samuel 3:12-16 talks about a strange reunion between David and Michal. Apparently Michal had been given to Paltiel as a wife when David fled from Saul and went into hiding. David would not take his throne until his proper claim (being married to the former King's daughter) was returned.

- Looking at the reaction of Paltiel, he seemed to truly love Michal. Describe what you imagine her heart might have been going through at this time? _____

_____

_____

_____

- During this reunion Michal is faced with the reality that she is just one of the wives now. However, she rightfully could stake her claim as the primary wife. 2 Samuel 5:13 tells of David's household increasing further with more wives and children, yet Michal had no children of her own. In ancient culture children carried on the lineage of the family and a great deal of importance was placed upon the shoulders of women to bear children in the family name.

- Try to imagine the awkwardness of Michal and David's reunion. Are there ever times of awkwardness when you are reunited with your spouse after a long separation? In what ways do you find it awkward? List ways to help ease the transition.

  1. Pray about the reunion beforehand.
  2. Pray together.
  3. Talk to each other about the fears and expectations.
  _____
  4. Re-establish family devotions.
  5. Discuss intimacy trepidations.
  6._____
  7._____
  8._____
  9._____
  10._____

- Do you ever allow anger to seep into your heart because you were left alone and left to take care of the children and the home, etc? Read Philippians 4:13, 19. How can you guard against those thoughts? Sometimes all it takes is for a wife to gently express her need for help from her husband when he gets home. However, keep in mind that the husband needs time to reacclimate to the lifestyle and roles in his home. In many cases he has been in a completely different culture that will affect his thinking and motivations. We on the home front must be willing to adjust our lifestyles, our hopes, and our desires to flexibly compromise with our spouses; otherwise we run the risk of becoming angry and bitter. Our needs can quickly turn to selfishness and pride that allows sin to seep into our marriage and cause dissonance. Humbly keep the lines of communication open and assume the best of your spouse._____
  _____
  _____
  _____

_____

_____

_____

5. Read 2 Samuel 6:12-23. In this passage we can clearly see the outward expression of bitterness rooted in Michal's heart. She either despised David for his passion to God or the way he expressed that joy. When we allow bitterness in our lives we are in a sense pointing a finger of blame at God for not giving us what we desire. Read Proverbs 14:10, Isaiah 38:17, Acts 8:23, Romans 3:14, Ephesians 4:31, and Hebrews 12:15. List the warnings, commands, and the promises about bitterness from these verses.

- Warnings: _____

_____

_____

_____

_____

_____

_____

- Commands:_____

_____

_____

_____

_____

_____

_____

- Promises:_____

_____

_____

_____

_____

_____

_____

6. Read 2 Samuel 6:20. Michal lashes out at David for the deep-seated passion he expressed to the Lord God. She betrays her bitterness and the Lord allows the writer here to call her "the daughter of Saul". God sovereignly ended the lineage of Saul and established David's heritage by not allowing Michal to have any children.

- Have you ever lashed out at your spouse (privately or publically) in a way that has erected a barrier in your relationship? List those situations and seek the Lord's forgiveness for your sin. Read 1 John 1:9 and Matthew 5:22-24. How can you apply these verses to your life and seek forgiveness from your spouse for your part in the issue? _____

  _____
  _____
  _____
  _____
  _____
  _____

- As wives, we tend to know how to push our husband's buttons better than anyone else. Which buttons rouse ire in your man? When you give in to the action of trying to improperly get a response from your spouse, how do your choices contradict Christlikeness (e.g., God is always kind; God is longsuffering)? Prayerfully ask the Lord's help to prevent yourself from pushing those buttons. Think through how you will respond in the future when you are tempted to do so, especially those times when both of you are under a large amount of stress. _____

  _____
  _____
  _____

- Read 1 Corinthians 13:3-8 and list each character trait that love (charity) exemplifies. Next to each trait write which ones you excel at and which ones you need to work on._____

  _____

_____

_____

_____

_____

_____

_____

_____

_____

7. What was the result of Michal's words? (Read 2 Samuel 6:23 and 1 Chronicles 15:29). Michal could have been respected and tenderly loved by David; however, instead of receiving a blessing from David she caustically criticized David's actions. _____

_____

_____

- David alludes to his claim to the throne because God gave it to him. He is humble in his rebuke but very truthful. Have you ever lost a blessing by refusing a gentle rebuke from your husband? Describe how you can biblically respond in the future by utilizing such passages as Psalm 10:12, 17; Proverbs 6:3; Proverbs 29:23; Matthew 18:4; Matthew 23:12; Colossians 3:11-13; James 4; and 1 Peter 5:5-7. _____

_____

_____

_____

_____

_____

8. Read the book of Esther. Compare and contrast Esther's situation with that of Michal. Both women were thrust into positions of power. Both had an opportunity to lie to protect themselves. Ponder

the blessings Esther received along with the blessings Michal for-feited because she let sin and bitterness into her soul.

• Compare

_____
_____
_____
_____
_____
_____
_____
_____
_____
_____

• Contrast

_____
_____
_____
_____
_____
_____
_____
_____
_____

9. Apply 1 John 1:9 to your life. Confess to the Lord any bitter-ness you may have towards your husband and ask for forgiveness. Prayerfully seek out your spouse and also seek his forgiveness for any sin against him in this area.

Chapter 3

A Woman of Power

Excerpts from the Diary of an Active Duty Female Soldier

04 April

Today my deployment schedule was confirmed. I agreed to postpone my request to leave active service so that I could go with my battalion to Afghanistan for another twelve - fourteen month deployment. This will be my third time in the Middle East and I am concerned for my safety every time I go, even if I am a behind-the-front-lines supply officer. If there's one thing I've learned from past tours to Iraq, it's that IEDs aren't picky. If it were just me to worry about I would not be so fearful. However, I hate leaving Jack. We have prayed about my staying in the military, and I think it is God's will, at least for now. We can't get married yet because of time restraints, and the decision to volunteer to go back to the desert was a tough one to make. Yet, the Lord has allowed me advancement and opportunity within the Army even if my heart is torn between the military and Jack! My heart aches for home more and more with each new separation, whether it's during month-long work-ups or year-long deployments. Now that I am engaged I really desire the whole wife/mom role. To be honest, the messages of Proverbs 31:10-31 and 1 Peter 3 are starting to challenge my thinking of women serving in the military. However, I must keep telling myself to persevere and finish out my contract with the government with honor. I must accomplish the task at hand. . .

08 April

Why are so many women I know disapproving of me? At prayer meeting tonight Jack mentioned that I will be deploying again soon and he asked people to pray that we have wisdom regarding the future. I actually heard Mrs. Jordan make a snide remark about a woman's place being at home, and I was sitting only a few rows in front of her. I wish she would have talked to me about it in private instead of throwing it out there in public the way that she did. Of course, I pretended not to hear her outburst and I put on the sweetest smile for her after the service ended, but sometimes I just wish I could make her understand. I know I need to graciously confront her on this, but I am hurt and offended and I don't want to make matters worse by approaching her with the wrong spirit. Don't people realize the struggle I go through? I guess my heart hurts because people know me so little. I talk to people at church, but none of the ladies go out of their way to befriend me. I guess I'm just too different for them. I don't know.

Yet, despite all I've gone through, the Lord is challenging many of my previous ambitions with Jack's help. When I joined the ROTC in high school I committed myself to becoming the best female officer ever. I've done very well, if I may say so myself! During my time in the service I have endured harassment, jealousy, unfair treatment, prejudice, and so much more. Then I met Jack at church when I moved to Fort Bragg. I don't know what I would do without him. I never thought I would *want* to be married, but he is my source of friendship and love. He approached me, befriended me, and the rest is history. He supports me in what I consider my ministry. I've been able to lead numerous women to the Lord, witness to countless others and disciple the women I come in contact with. I have a ministry with the men I work alongside with as well, but it's definitely different. Jack and I have had many conversations about why I'm in the military, when I want to get out, how marriage will change things, having kids, etc... Through these talks he's helped me realize that I must seek God's will for my life and not my own. This has been hard. I grew up thinking that a woman can do anything a man can. God has given me this special task to do right now but I am willing to humbly submit to what He wants me to do.

It still hurts, though, to know that so few women in my church even try to understand. I am in a lonely place right now, but I am thankful for the opportunity to serve my country. I know I am getting older and that I would like to have children. Yet, I've had a great career. Perhaps I could find a way to be an example to the young women in the military without having to continue to wear the uniform.

28 April

It's been a few weeks. I'm so excited about some of the opportunities I am going to have in Afghanistan. I always struggle with the fact that I have to leave Jack, but I really do get to do cool things. Anyway, my CO and I spoke one-on-one today and he was surprisingly supportive of some of my ideas about building camaraderie among the women. What a great day!

22 May

We're out in the field for training and it stinks – literally! I refuse to complain out loud, but it is miserable here. I miss my bed and my shower – ohhhhh, for a shower! And you know what is disgusting?! I still have men give me looks and hint at flirting. I can't stand it! I miss Jack. I guess these are just a few of the things I have to pretend I am used to. But I have gotten to know a few of the younger women here. Some are really rough around the edges but I can see the hurt and loneliness in their eyes. There is one whom I already see as trouble. She is cute and flirtatious – a dangerous combination for anyone. But I have to remind myself not to be judgmental. I know that the Lord can refine even the most unpolished individual; there is always more to these girls than meets the eye! Then there is the girl from Admin, Jay. She reminds me so much of myself when I was young. And she doesn't tolerate anything the guys try to pull. She is searching and asking great questions. This is why I am still here! These girls need a military mother's care, and I just humbly seek God's help to make the right decisions. Thank you, Lord, for the reminders, and help me to bring these women to you!

The Biblical Background

Many books have been written about the role of women in the family and society, but Christians should look to the Bible to guide our thinking here, as in every other aspect of life. Important passages to study regarding this topic are the books of Ruth and Esther, Proverbs 31, 1 Corinthians 7, 1 Timothy 2:9-15, Titus 2 and 1 Peter 3.

Meditation Passage: Judges 5:31a

Focal Passage: Read Judges 4 and 5

1. Deborah is a judge and prophetess in Israel. Judges 4:8 reveals that Barak refuses to obey the command of God without Deborah's presence in combat. Verse 9 gives Deborah's answer. Write out this verse in your own words. Also note that this passage does not say that Deborah fought in the battle, but that Barak oversaw the fighting forces (vv. 14-15, 22). _____

_____

_____

_____

- Deborah's response shows courage and faith in God. What do you think is the role of courage and faith in a leader's decision process? _____

_____

_____

_____

- Barak obeyed but with prompting (4:8, 9, 14). Hebrews 11:32 mentions Barak's faith. He might have desired Deborah to go with him as he boldly carried out the seemingly impossible battle. Reflect on Genesis 32:24-32 and 2 Kings 2:1-15. Jacob and Elisha both requested difficult but specific blessings from God. How could Barak's response compared with these two men? Describe the different leadership styles you have witnessed during your spouse's involvement in the military. Are some styles more suitable than others? Is there one style that is better than another? _____

_____

_____

_____

_____

_____

_____

- Deborah took charge and delegated responsibility to Barak and the army in verse 14. What power does a leader have through delegation? _____

_____

_____

_____

_____

_____

_____

2. We meet Jael in Judges 4:18. Here we find a woman who was cunning and resourceful. She kept her wits about her, even under pressure, and God used her to kill the captain of Jabin's army, Sisera. This act of courage ended the battle, and God gave Israel peace for forty years. Deborah's prophecy in Judges 4:9 states that Sisera would fall at the hand of a woman. Which woman do you think it is referring to? Deborah or Jael? Why? _____

_____

_____

_____

_____

_____

_____

3. Judges 5:7, 15 speak of Deborah as a presence throughout this battle. What is your view towards women in the military, politics, or important leadership roles? Is the Bible clear on this subject?_____

_____

_____

_____

_____

_____

_____

- How does this passage shed light on women in leadership?

  _____

  _____

  _____

- Deborah gives God the glory in verse 9. As a Christian woman, you have been redeemed by Christ, and your achievements must be given to Him. What is the proper balance between giving God the glory and also knowing who you are and what you are capable of? What does Philippians 2:13 say about where the desire to do God's will and the ability to do it comes from? _____

  _____

  _____

  _____

  _____

  _____

- Does this passage imply that the Lord sanctions women to have leadership positions within the military or government? How does our culture view women in secular positions of leadership? What does your church teach about women's roles in public service? Does this contrast with passages regarding the mother and wife's role in the home (Proverbs 31, 1 Timothy 3, 1 Peter 3, Colossians 3, Ephesians 5, 1 Corinthians 7)? Is it possible for a woman to carry out her God-given duties to her family while serving in the military?_____

_____

_____

_____

_____

_____

_____

- Write out a prayer for the women in uniform.

_____

_____

_____

_____

_____

_____

- What unique issues do you think a woman in uniform faces? What are some ways you can try to encourage her? (If you serve as a woman in uniform, personalize this question.)

_____

_____

_____

_____

_____

_____

- Read Proverbs 31. There is an age old difference of opinion about women working outside the home. Compare and contrast a woman in uniform to a full-time working mom.

  o Compare

_____

_____

_____

_____

_____

_____

○ Contrast

_____

_____

_____

_____

_____

_____

4. Actively seek out ways to encourage women in uniform. You can do this through prayer, support for her family while she is deployed, or simply by being a friend. Judges 5:31a is a great prayer for a woman in uniform. Write it out and memorize the verse. _____

_____

_____

_____

_____

Chapter 4

Second Chances

Dear Diary,

I get so tired of all the abuse I deal with. Rex is supposed to love me and cherish me. He is so very careful to leave bruises where no one can see them. But the true pain is within. All his friends always comment on how wonderful, beautiful, able, etc. I am, but that only incites his anger against me even more. I try so hard to practice 1 Peter 3:1-6: submitting to my husband, reflecting on the inner spirit, doing good and trying not to fear. I try so hard, but some days I feel like it is impossible. Can I really stay with him even one more day? Oh, Lord, please help me! I don't know if I can go on!

Dear Diary,

Things have been somewhat better lately. Rex goes through phases and he seems to be on an upswing right now. He didn't even get mad the other day when one of his friends commented on me being the perfect wife. Rex just puffed up his chest a little more and took it as a compliment to him. I quietly gave praise to the Lord. Thank you, Lord! You always send hope just when I think I can't keep going.

Dear Diary,

I have a confession. I sometimes daydream that Rex dies and I have freedom again. He makes plenty of money, so it's not that I *need* anything. Well, I don't need anything that requires money. But would it hurt for him to say a kind word to me every now and then? I try in every way possible to please him and take care of him. He certainly doesn't deserve it, but I don't deserve God's love either.

I hate it when he wants to have sex with me. I feel used and disgusting. It's as if he is raping me. But he's my husband, so it's not rape, right? Just a rape of my soul! Ughhh.

I feel worthless and useless as a woman. What if I died? He wouldn't even care. In fact he would probably find the next young thing to woo and then forget all about her too. I'm complaining again. Lord, forgive me and help me keep hope. I need you so much. Help!

Dear Diary,

He had sex with me last night. I have the bruises to prove it. I can't pretend I'm okay today, so I'm staying in my room. I tried so hard to submit and not fight him, but he is so different from what he should be. It feels like my life is over before it's really begun. Where is the "happy ever after" I dreamed of? I don't think I can go on.

A few months later . . .

Dear Diary,

I'm sad to say that I am relieved. Rex died yesterday. It sounds heartless to say, but I feel like I have been set free from years of slavery. But then, should I have tried harder? I'm glad to be free, but I still grieve for my dreams that will never be. . . There is a pang of sorrow knowing he never knew the Lord, yet he was a worthless man who set himself up as his own god. He is gone and I am free. Now I wonder at who I am. I'm supposed to be a Christian but how does a Christian find joy in such a horrible thing. He's dead, I'm free, but my heart is broken nonetheless.

Six months later . . .

Dear Diary,

Strange to say but I have met someone. Steve's in the military and seems to really love the Lord. In fact, it has been some time since I've met anyone with such a commanding presence. Everything about him exudes confidence in the Lord.

I met Steve at a local community event that our church partici- pated in. His unit was also involved and we completely hit it off. He was so bold and straightforward, but not in a shameful way. He asked me for my number and called me the next day. We will be going out in a couple of nights. I wonder what the Lord has in store for me? It's so soon after Rex died, but I am willing to start a rela- tionship if it is God's will.

Dear Diary,

Steve does not mince words or motives. He told me on our date that he is a man of decision and that he has already begun praying about us getting married. I recoiled at first. Rex still haunts my memory, but by the end of the conversation he was making sense. I need to commit this to prayer. Do I really want to be married again? I used to dream what it would be like to marry someone who could respect and appreciate me. Maybe the Lord is granting the desire of my heart in this very unusual way.

Six months later . . .

Dear Diary,

We are getting married tomorrow. Steve and I have not known each other for too long, but we have prayed about our decision, sought out counsel, and are getting married. We don't know every- thing about each other but we can learn as we go. I'm indebted to the Lord. I'm nervous but I'm also so grateful, just so very grateful! God has given me a second chance.

The Biblical Background

Prior to his ascension to the throne of Israel, David and his mighty men spent much of their time as vagabonds. They travelled throughout the land trying to stay away from Saul and maintain a livelihood for themselves. It was during this time that David made a simple request to Nabal, asking for food for his men. Nabal refused the appeal, and insulted David, even though David and his men had provided protection for Nabal's servants. David became angry, and set out to get revenge against Nabal.

Meditation Passage: 1 Peter 3:1-6

Focal Passage: Read 1 Samuel 25

1. Samuel 25 begins after an important person's death. Who was it that died? How did this man's death influence David? Have you lost someone who served as your spiritual mentor? What is their legacy to you? _____

_____

_____

_____

_____

_____

- David and Saul were at peace but David remained in the wilderness. Imagine the difficulties involved with finding food, shelter, and protection in the wilderness for a large group of people. Modern day military members often face similar challenges. Write a list of comparisons between David and a person deployed._____

  _____

  _____

  _____

  _____

- Also write out a list of problems you think a deployed person struggles with (such as boredom, loneliness, etc.). A large portion of the book of Psalms is penned by David in these times of wilderness. Seek out passages of encouragement in the Psalms of David to memorize and share with deployed service members to encourage them in the Lord. _____

_____

_____

_____

_____

_____

_____

- During this time, Michal was given to another man in marriage. What effect do you think this had on David? _____

_____

_____

2. We are introduced to Nabal for the first time in 1 Samuel 25. Describe Nabal in your own words (his name means "worthless").

_____

_____

_____

- There are many godly women and men who are married to ungodly people. What does 1 Corinthians 7:10-16 and Matthew 5:32 say about divorce? Does God ever give a way out of the covenant of marriage if you are married to an ungodly or difficult individual? What do these passages say could happen if a saved person stays in such a marriage (1 Corinthians 7:14, 16)? _____

_____

_____

_____

_____

_____

_____

3. The Bible describes Abigail as discerning. What is the definition of discernment? Do you have this quality? What are some practical ways to develop this characteristic in your life? Read through 1 Samuel 25 again and focus on the actions of Abigail. _____

_____

_____

_____

_____

_____

_____

- How did others respond to her?

  o The servants _____

    _____

    _____

  o David_____

    _____

    _____

  o Nabal_____

    _____

    _____

- Other than discernment, what other qualities does Abigail display in this passage? Start with the list below and add any others you might find. Give a brief definition for each and include Bible verses that deal with them. You might want to start with Proverbs 31; Colossians 3:18-25; Ephesians 5:22-29; 1 Timothy 3:10-12; 1 Timothy 4:6-8; and 1 Peter 3:1-3, noting the qualities you need to work on. Prayerfully seek to grow in these areas.

  o <u>Approachable</u>_____

  o <u>Loyal</u>_____

  o <u>Provider</u>_____

- o Giver _____
- o Quick to do What is Right _____
- o Peacekeeper _____
- o Hard Worker _____
- o Honoring _____
- o Patient _____
- o Courageous _____
- o Faith in God _____
- o Gracious Speech _____
- o _____
- o _____
- o _____
- o _____
- o _____
- o _____
- o _____
- o _____
- o _____
- o _____
- o _____
- o _____
- o _____

• Abigail's actions protected her husband and servants, while at the same time stopping David from acting foolishly. Abigail honored Nabal even when he did not deserve it. But in a sense she also acted out from under Nabal's authority by going to David. Keeping Matthew 19:1-9 and Mark 10:1-12 in mind, how can you encourage someone in a difficult marriage to persevere amidst extreme hardship by using Abigail as an example? _____

_____
_____
_____
_____
_____
_____

4. Abigail was quick to accept David's offer of marriage. Looking at
1 Samuel 25, list the qualities David saw in Abigail and vice versa.

_____
_____
_____
_____
_____
_____

- What was David's occupation as a child and young man?
  Nabal shepherded, therefore Abigail was familiar with the
  various aspects involved with raising sheep and goats. Did
  this shared background give David and Abigail a common
  reference point in their marriage? How does a similar background (whether it is cultural, socio-economic, racial, reli-
  gious, etc.) help you build a firm foundation in a relationship?

_____
_____
_____
_____
_____
_____

- Both David and Abigail suffered heartache from their previous marriages. Read Philippians 3:13-14. How can one
  move beyond the past and accept the gracious gift of a new
  partner? What are some things David and Abigail may have
  appreciated about one another because of their individual past
  experiences? What stability do you think they had in their
  marriage even when they would be separated or bombarded
  by outward stressors? _____

_____
_____
_____
_____
_____
_____

- Keep in mind that this was not as wonderful an escape as it initially appeared. David took another wife at nearly the same time. Abigail's life with David was as one of the many wives, fraught with danger, kidnapping, and drama.

5. Read the additional passages referring to David and Abigail's relationship (1 Samuel 30:5, 18-20; 2 Samuel 2:1-3; 3:3). It is interesting to note that Abigail's children are never mentioned as getting entangled by sin like David's other sons. How can a mom who faithfully strives to live a godly life for her children take encouragement from this? _____

_____
_____
_____
_____

6. 1 Samuel 25:29 is a wonderful verse to pray for a man in uniform. Write out the verse, memorize it, and then pray it for those you know who serve our military. _____

_____
_____
_____
_____

Chapter 5

Ultimate Betrayal

Her Side:

The counselor says that I need to write out my thoughts in order to help address the problems facing my marriage. So here I go.

Eddie and I are separated and we have both agreed to see a counselor. I really don't want a divorce, but I don't think Eddie will ever forgive me. In fact, I don't know if I can forgive myself. We have a Christian counselor. (Both Eddie and I are "Christians".) We both grew up "in" the church and have been faithful in attending together whenever he's home. But while he was gone on a year-long deployment to the Middle East, Jason overwhelmed me. He was passionate and dominating. I don't think I was looking for a relationship – or was I? You see, Eddie and I have been married for two years now. He deployed for the first time just after we had been married for slightly less than a year. We dated, got engaged, and then married within a whirlwind 4 months. I never expected that we would be going through this. I am so young. How could I go and ruin everything?

Jason is also in the military. He's quite a few ranks higher than Eddie and I guess I was mesmerized by that. He was here in the States while Eddie was gone. We met at the gym a few times and then would run into each other at other places. But meeting at the gym became a regular habit. Then one morning he asked if I wanted to join him for breakfast at a fast food place. I never thought it could lead to an affair. He was so concerned for me and we even talked frequently about Eddie. We ended up going to breakfast regularly. In my heart I could feel that I was pulling away from Eddie and I stopped attending church because I felt guilty. But I didn't want to stop the friendship with Jason. He was handsome. He was "there." He seemed to understand things like no one else could, and he would always say something that seemed so profound. What's more, he would tell me things that were sort of "confidential." Now I realize that it was probably more of a ploy to pull me in more.

No one knows how lonely I was. Eddie couldn't call or email much. He was just trying to stay alive. I thought he just didn't care for me. I told myself that to convince myself I wasn't doing so much wrong. Then, one day, Jason reached out and touched my hand at breakfast and then held it. I hadn't felt so alive in a long time. Everything in me told me to run as fast as I could out of there. I just couldn't bring myself to let go. I didn't go to the gym the next day and Jason called to check on me. I don't know how he got my phone number. I didn't give it to him. I just told him I was confused. He said he understood and that he would try to stay away. The next time we saw each other was at the gym a week later. It was awkward but he came over to try to make me feel like it wasn't so strange. I had missed him and we ended up at breakfast again. Then later in the week he asked if I wanted to go to dinner with him. I stared at him and said that I couldn't be seen with him in public like that. He offered to make me dinner at his apartment. Why did I say yes? I got there and was so scared. I knew I should just run but I couldn't. He put me at ease and then by the end of the night we had sex. I stayed with him all night and pretended it didn't bother me. But I really felt like trash. It was not special like it had been with Eddie. In fact, the feeling afterward was like having the flu deep down inside my heart.

I remember when it hit me that I had to tell Eddie. He called because he had just lost a buddy who was shot. He was devastated and said he just had to hear my voice. I cried and cried out of guilt. He probably thought it was because I missed him. I was convicted. I truly repented, prayed and prayed, and then I called Jason and told him it was over. He begged and pleaded with me not to let it end. He offered to house me until the divorce finalized and then marry me. He even threatened to make Eddie's life harder. But all of the reasons I had been drawn to him seemed incredibly lame, and I suddenly knew that he wasn't as powerful as he said he was. I switched gyms. I refused to answer his calls. The one time he stopped by my apartment I told him to leave or I'd call the cops or go to the military police and really make his life miserable. I wouldn't say anything more and shut the door in his face. Yet I had to tell Eddie and I didn't know how or what would happen.

I called my deacon's wife at church and asked her to meet with me. When she did, I poured out the whole story and asked for her help. Eddie was due to be home in just 3 weeks so I was unsure if I should tell him by letter or phone or what. She and her husband assured me that they would prayerfully help us out anyway they could. We thought that it would be best to wait until he was home to confess since he was in such a dangerous situation. During those weeks I sought the Lord like I had never done before. I went through a purging and cleansing process. And as hard as it was I put the whole situation in the Lord's hands. I did not know what Eddie would want to do. He had every right to divorce me and it hurt me so much that I had caused it.

Eddie returned, and was instantly aware that something wasn't right. When we got home I sat him down on the couch and told him everything. He was strangely quiet and said nothing. It scared me. I told him I had already arranged to stay at the deacon's house with his family until Eddie could decide what he wanted to do. I got my bag and I left. Eddie didn't try to stop me. He didn't say anything. He didn't cry or flinch in my presence. He let me walk out of there without so much as a word.

That was 2 months ago. We've really only communicated through the counselor and the deacon. Eddie will speak to the deacon and the counselor, but he said he's just not ready to talk to me yet. This was the first assignment that the counselor wanted us to do. I'm very discouraged at this point. I know I deserve to reap what I have sown. Just because I have taken a few steps in the right direction and repented doesn't mean that God will take away the consequences of my actions.

I also realize now that I was still kind of acting like I was dating even though I was married. I thought it was still okay to be close friends with the opposite sex instead of developing that deeper relationship with Eddie. I wanted to be young and free to do whatever. I regret it now. I really needed to grow up and take our marriage seriously.

I have to add that I truly want this marriage to work. I feel like I have grown so much in such a short time – the extremely hard way. I don't know if I can ever be worthy of Eddie again but I know I can strive to be the best wife God will enable me to be. I hate the thought of being a failure in this most important area in my life. But I hate that I have hurt the man I truly love more than anything. I just hope Eddie can forgive me even if he can't stay with me. I understand him not desiring me right now too. I long for him to touch me again. I almost feel like it would be kind of like a cleansing process for him to want to be intimate again. I wish I could go back and change it all but I can't. I love Eddie but I love God more. I want to do what is right even if it is hard.

His Side:

I was completely blindsided by Mary's confession. I seriously had no inclination that she was anything but faithful to me. It had never even crossed my mind that she could ever cheat on me. I know our romance was a whirlwind, but we were drawn to each other instantly. We shared the deepest parts of our souls to each other and knew that marriage was the only way to live. It was hard being deployed so soon after we were married. In many ways we weren't prepared for such a separation that quickly. It didn't help that I was in a remote area with little access to the modern electronic forms of communication. Calling home was an infrequent opportunity. We wrote to each other. She wrote to me more, but I just didn't have time. I saw many buddies of mine injured and a few were killed. I can't talk about it still. When I told her about Jack dying I thought she, of all people, would understand my torn heart. Now I find out that she was with "him" during that time.

I have never been away from the church for long. This experience has certainly shown me that I haven't had much of a relationship with the Lord either. I look at Mary and I am torn in two. I can see she has changed. But she hurt me on a level akin to watching Jack die. Only she was my soul mate.

I couldn't talk to her that night. I had just returned home with all the hopes of reuniting with my wife. I guess I can understand her waiting until I got home to tell me. There really is no good time to drop a bomb on someone. But she has to understand what I was going through. All of my expectations and hopes were shattered all at once. I had just spent an entire year defending myself with weapons. At least in the field I had body armor and a helmet to protect me. My buddies had my back. At home my heart was totally exposed and vulnerable - I truly wanted to die when she told me. Then I became enraged at that guy for trapping my wife, and then it turned into complete anger to Mary for her betrayal. I did not trust myself. I had many dark thoughts of anger and murder and rage going through my mind. I had to sit there and just be quiet. I am sure she wanted me to respond in some way but those dark thoughts scared me to death. I didn't move for hours. What Mary probably doesn't know is that night I ended up on my knees in a much needed conversation with God. I needed time. I needed prayer.

I agreed to speak to the deacon. Praise the Lord for such a man! He has carefully guided me to particular passages in the Bible to help me understand God's position in all of this. But every time I think of trying to talk to Mary it's like my heart is ready to bleed all over again and I can't do it. The deacon and his wife recommended us seeking counseling. I have nothing to lose and everything to gain – maybe even a relationship with Mary again. I don't think I have seriously considered divorcing Mary, but I can't imagine touching her again after knowing she has been with someone else. I have a lot I need to learn about being a godly leader in our home. I'm willing to see where the Lord will lead in all of this but Mary is going to have to be patient. I have much that I am carrying from being deployed and this is a stress beyond any I've known. But I do know that I have hope. I do have hope in God.

The Biblical Background

Divorce and remarriage is discussed in Malachi 2:16, Matthew 19:6-9, Deuteronomy 24:1-4, Matthew 5:32 and 1 Corinthians 7:15. Passages on adultery and fornication include Exodus 20:14, Matthew 5:27-28, Matthew 5:32, Matthew 19:9, 18, Mark 10:11-12, Luke 16:18, 1 Corinthians 6, Galatians 5:21, Ephesians 5:3-5 and Hebrews 13:4. All of these Scriptures should be considered while studying David's relationship with Bathsheba.

Meditation Passage: Proverbs 24:6

Focal Passage: 2 Samuel 11 and 12

1. 2 Samuel 11:1 gives a very telling commentary about David. David is supposed to be out on the battlefield.

- Where is he? _____
- Thinking about David's position and all the war he had seen, can you imagine his desire to stay at home instead of facing the battles again? _____
- Do even the best military leaders get exhausted and become weak to temptation? _____
  _____
  _____

- Using biblical principles (give references if you can), what would you say to encourage David to do right at the end of verse 1? _____
  _____
  _____

- The military leaders over your loved one have many responsibilities on their shoulders. It is our duty to pray that the Lord will protect them from sin and give them wisdom to do right. List the commands from 1Timothy 2:1-4, Psalm 119:98-100 and Romans 13:1-6. _____

_____
_____
_____
_____
_____
_____

2. Read 2 Samuel 11:2-3 and write a description of Bathsheba.

_____
_____
_____

- Verse 4 gives rise to much debate on Bathsheba's guilt in this whole affair. What do you think went through Bathsheba's mind when she was sent for by the King? _____

  _____
  _____
  _____
  _____
  _____
  _____

- Put yourself in her shoes. Would you rush to your spouse's Commanding Officer if he called you out of the blue? ___

  _____
  _____
  _____
  _____

- Would you think that it is an important message from your husband? Could there be a sense of anticipation for some good news, or worse, bad news? _____

  _____
  _____
  _____
  _____

- When she came into the king's presence and realized the reason for the summons, what do you think went through her mind? _____

_____

_____

_____

_____

_____

_____

3. Verse 4 also tells us that Bathsheba was purified from her uncleanness. This is saying among other things that she had just finished her period and was, in essence, able to get pregnant. After the sinful act with David she returned to her house.

- Do you think David was completely at fault (almost guilty of rape?) _____

_____

_____

_____

- Cross reference your answers with 2 Samuel 11:26, 12:9-10. God continues to call Bathsheba "the wife of Uriah" until after David's confession and repentance. _____

_____

_____

_____

_____

_____

_____

4. Uriah was a Hittite and one of David's "mighty men."
- Read 2 Samuel 11:7-17 and 2 Samuel 23 to see the impressive qualifications of David's "mighty men." Was Uriah worthy of honor? _____

_____

_____
_____
_____

- What qualities do you see in him that are honorable? _____

  _____
  _____
  _____
  _____
  _____
  _____

- Uriah would not enjoy the comforts of home or be intimate with Bathsheba because he knew his duty was on the battlefield. Is there a possibility that this heaped even more guilt on David for not going to the battlefield? _____

  _____
  _____
  _____

- Read Romans 13:1-6, 1 Corinthians 9:27, and Titus 3:1-3. What example does Uriah's behavior give of how a soldier may enjoy some refreshment while still bearing his position and responsibility? _____

  _____
  _____
  _____
  _____
  _____
  _____

5. 2 Samuel 11:26 tells us Bathsheba's plight.

- Can you imagine the mourning in her soul over Uriah's death? Her guilt in adultery and being pregnant? Summarize in your own words the many different emotions Bathsheba must have been experiencing. _____

_____
_____
_____

- Verse 27 goes on to tell us that David brought Bathsheba into his harem and married her. Do you think she might have felt guilty, used, abused, forsaken, hurt, etc.? Search for Bible passages on the comfort and peace of God, and write down verses you could give to someone who is suffering. (2 Corinthians 1:3-4 and Colossians 2:2). _____

_____
_____
_____
_____
_____
_____
_____
_____

- Look at 2 Samuel 12:18. What added grief did Bathsheba face?

_____
_____
_____

6. Notice that Bathsheba is not referred to as David's wife until 2 Samuel 12:24. 2 Samuel 11 and 12 narrates the story of David's sin. Psalm 51 is the psalm of repentance that David wrote after his sin of adultery and murder. Write out Psalm 51 noting the process that David went through to repent, forsake his sin, and seek restitution.

_____
_____
_____
_____
   ·
_____
_____
_____
_____

_____
_____
_____

7. In reference to the specific situation with Bathsheba and David, David was guilty of the sin, and he brought Bathsheba into it. Look at Matthew 5:31-32 and describe the responsibility of the man in reference to adultery and divorce. _____
_____
_____
_____
_____

8. Is it possible that David's actions and repentance enabled Bathsheba to also heal and move on from the experience? Read 2 Samuel 12:24. Consider the intimacy that might have occurred due to David's comfort and the rejoicing over a second son being born to them, one who remained alive. _____
_____
_____

9. 2 Kings 1 and 2 describe Bathsheba as being the queen, and her son Solomon receiving the throne from David. In spite of her experiences, good or bad, God put Bathsheba in a place of honor and power for His glory. Looking at the life of Bathsheba, what comfort can you give to someone who has gravely sinned yet repented from their actions? Write out Philippians 3:13. _____
_____
_____
_____
_____
_____

10. Forgiveness is an amazing, special, and unique gift from our Savior. He forgives our sins and we can, therefore, forgive others

when they sin against us. Look at the following verses and give a brief description of the forgiveness from the Lord:

- Psalm 130:4 _____
- Daniel 9:9 _____
- Matthew 26:28 _____
- Luke 1:76-77 _____
- Luke 24:46-47 _____
- John 20:23 _____
- Acts 2:38 _____
- Acts 5:31 _____
- Acts 10:43 _____
- Ephesians 1:7 _____
- Ephesians 4:31-32 _____
- Colossians 1:14 _____
- 1 John 1:7 _____

11. Unfortunately, adultery is a common sin that occurs within the military community.
- What specific temptations tempt spouses into extra-marital affairs? _____
_____
_____
_____

- Name the problems a woman could get into by pursuing a close relationship with a man while her husband is deployed?
_____
_____
_____
_____

- Reflect on Philippians 4:4-9. How can you guard your heart against affairs and how can you encourage others around you to guard their hearts? _____
_____

_____

_____

- If you are a spouse who has been betrayed by unfaithfulness, how does God make it possible for you to learn to forgive and trust again? (Look at the passages from question #10 on forgiveness.)

    o Write out steps to take to begin to heal.
    o Read Psalm 51 again and consider if there is some-thing you need to repent of in the situation, and/or how you should respond if your spouse is repentant.
    o Pray for the Holy Spirit's help to enable you to for-give your spouse as often as is necessary.
    o Ask God to comfort you, and give you grace as He works His will in you and in your spouse.
    o Be willing to work hard to save your marriage.

- Write out a commitment to the Lord to remain faithful to your spouse both mentally and physically. Focus on Matthew 5:27-29, Genesis 2:24, Matthew 19:4-6, and Mark 10:6-8.

_____

_____

_____

_____

_____

_____

_____

_____

_____

_____

_____

_____

- God's grace pours out to the thirsty soul facing the daily task of striving to live in this world while not being part of it (John 17:15). All of us fail. None of us can earn a good life or a good marriage just by following steps and doing right. That's the beauty of the gospel and the glory of salvation. Reflect on Psalm 86 and cry out to God as the Psalmist did. Look up the following passages on God's grace and choose a few of them to commit to memory. Ephesians 2:8-9, Romans 3:23-24, Romans 5:1-2, 1 Corinthians 15:10.

• Talk to your spouse about boundaries you will both set and write them down. For example, "I will not be alone at any time with someone of the opposite sex." _____

_____

_____

_____

_____

_____

_____

_____

Chapter 6

Different Situations for Us All

Jane has been married for over 25 years and has never known her husband, Bill, outside of the military. Now the time for retirement has come and, quite frankly, she doesn't know what she is going to do with Bill underfoot all the time. He wants to take time off and she wants to go to work. All the kids are in college and they know they have some serious adjusting to do.

Elisa and Jorge have been married for two months and are loving life together. Jorge will soon go out to sea for six months and Elisa cries every night because she can't believe he'll be gone for so long. Jorge is beside himself trying to figure out how to help Elisa. It bothers him that he is leaving, but he's used to the lifestyle. He's been in the Coast Guard for four years now and is fairly established. He struggles knowing how to help Elisa. Elisa gets frustrated knowing she can't stop herself from crying.

Bryan is divorced with a lot of baggage from his first wife. She had an affair while he was deployed, took his two kids back to their home town, and remarried in a very short amount of time. He doesn't feel like he should fight for custody – yet. Amy is falling in love with him but she was reared in a Christian home and just doesn't know how to proceed. Does she allow herself to marry him? Does she cut it off before she gets in too deep?

Elaine and George have been married for about six years. George has been in the military the entire time. They have always been able to make moves together in the past, but George recently got orders to report to a new base from which he will soon deploy. He will not be able to help Elaine sell their current home and assist her in the move to the new location. George is overwhelmed by what he has to accomplish in a very short amount of time, while Elaine is overwhelmed by the tasks she must complete without George's help and input. She understands this is all part of the military, but she has never had to do it herself and is desperate for the Lord's help.

Michaela joined the Army Reserves. She is in her late 20's, single, and has a good head on her shoulders. She is figuring out very quickly that most of the married men are willing to ignore their wedding vows for a chance to be with her. She is fresh meat to them. But she has a strong foundation in the Lord and can stand on her own two feet. She gets lonely, though, and really needs encouragement in the Lord!

Belinda's youngest son is overseas. She's middle aged and has no previous experience with the military. She knows that her son is safest in the will of God but would really like to be educated about much more regarding life in the military. Her son uses acronyms that she doesn't understand (even though he does try to write out what they mean). She sends letters that are sometimes returned and tries desperately not to panic. She doesn't live anywhere close to any bases and feels like she is out of the loop.

There are so many scenarios that people can face when dealing with the military. The Bible may not always have a clear Biblical account to apply to the specific situation at hand, but there are many opportunities to glean helpful applications and hope from various people in Scripture and the wonderful overarching theme of grace to apply to all situations. This last chapter will give you an opportunity to look at people that may not have transparent military connections, but help us understand God's position on how to respond to different situations we may face. Often we see great men and don't consider, or even know how their wives, children, or parents dealt with drastic life changes. Try to place yourself in each person's situation and prayerfully consider your response to these stories.

Passages will Vary for Each Situation

1. Read Joshua 1:14, 11:23. The wives and children mentioned here grew up during the forty year pilgrimage in the wilderness and watched their husbands fight to gain their land. Now they had to establish brand new lives in a foreign environment while their husbands left to help the remaining Israelite tribes conquer their lands.

- Who are the main characters? _____
  _____
  _____
  _____

- What other characters may be "unseen"? (Think of family members of these characters and how you would respond if you were transported back into history into this situation.)
  _____
  _____
  _____
  _____

- Which character traits are exemplary and should be used as a pattern for contemporary Christian living? _____
  _____
  _____
  _____
  _____
  _____

- Which character traits are unchristian and should be avoided or purged from a Christian's life? _____
  _____
  _____
  _____
  _____
  _____

- What is the crisis (or crises) faced? _____

_____

_____

_____

- What is the proper Biblical response in this situation?

_____

_____

_____

_____

_____

_____

- HowcanIapplythistomylifeifIamfacedwithasimilarsituation?

_____

_____

_____

_____

_____

- How can I encourage or rebuke others through what I have learned? _____

_____

_____

_____

_____

_____

- How is grace shown through this story? _____

_____

_____

_____

_____

• In what way is the gospel revealed through this situation?

_____
_____
_____
_____
_____
_____

2. Read Joshua 2. Rahab begins as a harlot in Jericho only to join the Israelite nation as they continue on in conquest of the Promised Land. She is in the line of Christ and is honored in Hebrews 11 for her faith.

• Who are the main characters? _____

_____
_____
_____

• What other characters may be "unseen"? (Think of family members of these characters and how you would respond if you were transported back into history into this situation.)

_____
_____
_____
_____

• Which character traits are exemplary and should be used as a pattern for contemporary Christian living? _____

_____
_____
_____
_____

• Which character traits are unchristian and should be avoided or purged from a Christian's life? _____

_____

_____
_____
_____
_____

- What is the crisis (or crises) faced? _____
_____
_____
_____

- What is the proper Biblical response in this situation?
_____
_____
_____
_____
_____

- How can I apply this to my life if I am faced with a similar situation? _____
_____
_____
_____
_____
_____

- How can I encourage or rebuke others through what I have learned? _____
_____
_____
_____
_____
_____

- How is grace shown through this story? _____

  _____

  _____

  _____

  _____

  _____

- In what way is the gospel revealed through this situation?

  _____

  _____

  _____

  _____

  _____

3. Read Joshua 14:6-15; 15:14-19; Judges 1:12-20. Caleb's daughter Achsah grew up in a military home and also married into the military. Consider her submission, her stamina, and her boldness.

- Who are the main characters? _____

  _____

  _____

- What other characters may be "unseen"? (Think of family members of these characters and how you would respond if you were transported back into history into this situation.)

  _____

  _____

  _____

  _____

- Which character traits are exemplary and should be used as a pattern for contemporary Christian living? _____

  _____

  _____

_____
_____
_____

- Which character traits are unchristian and should be avoided or purged from a Christian's life? _____

_____
_____
_____
_____
_____

- What is the crisis (or crises) faced? _____

_____
_____
_____

- What is the proper Biblical response in this situation? _____

_____
_____
_____
_____
_____
_____

- How can I apply this to my life if I am faced with a similar situation? _____

_____
_____
_____
_____
_____
_____

- How can I encourage or rebuke others through what I have learned? _____

_____
_____
_____
_____
_____
_____

• How is grace shown through this story? _____
_____
_____
_____
_____
_____

• In what way is the gospel revealed through this situation?
_____
_____
_____
_____
_____

4. Read Judges 11:1-40. Jephthah was a mighty warrior who made a rash vow that affected his family. As the son of a prostitute, his half brothers forced him away from his home so he would not have an inheritance from his father. When war loomed close, his half brothers beckoned him to return to lead war against the Ammonites. Jephthah agreed and went to war; however, he made a vow to the Lord that greatly affected his legacy. Jephthah's daughter shows obedience, strength, and courage in honoring her father's vow to the Lord. (The reaction of Jephthah's daughter going to the mountains to bemoan her virginity suggests that she honored the vow by never getting married or bearing children to carry on the family heritage, not that Jephthah sacrificed her.) Jephthah is again mentioned in Hebrews 11.

- Who are the main characters? _____
  _____
  _____
  _____

- What other characters may be "unseen"? (Think of family members of these characters and how you would respond if you were transported back into history into this situation.)
  _____
  _____
  _____
  _____

- Which character traits are exemplary and should be used as a pattern for contemporary Christian living? _____
  _____
  _____
  _____
  _____
  _____

- Which character traits are unchristian and should be avoided or purged from a Christian's life? _____
  _____
  _____
  _____
  _____
  _____

- What is the crisis (or crises) faced? _____
  _____
  _____
  _____

- What is the proper Biblical response in this situation?
  _____

_____

_____

_____

_____

_____

- How can I apply this to my life if I am faced with a similar situation? _____

_____

_____

_____

_____

_____

- How can I encourage or rebuke others through what I have learned? _____

_____

_____

_____

_____

_____

- How is grace shown through this story? _____

_____

_____

_____

_____

_____

- In what way is the gospel revealed through this situation?

_____

_____

_____

_____
_____
_____

5. Read Matthew 8:5-13 and Luke 7:1-10. The Centurion was a great military leader and a man of faith. The Jews respected him and asked the Lord to help him. Think of how the Centurion's wife and family responded to the situation.

- Who are the main characters? _____
  _____
  _____
  _____

- What other characters may be "unseen"? (Think of family members of these characters and how you would respond if you were transported back into history into this situation.)
  _____
  _____
  _____
  _____

- Which character traits are exemplary and should be used as a pattern for contemporary Christian living? _____
  _____
  _____
  _____
  _____
  _____

- Which character traits are unchristian and should be avoided or purged from a Christian's life? _____
  _____
  _____
  _____
  _____
  _____

- What is the crisis (or crises) faced? _____
  _____
  _____
  _____
  _____
  _____
  _____

- What is the proper Biblical response in this situation?
  _____
  _____
  _____
  _____
  _____
  _____

- How can I apply this to my life if I am faced with a similar situation? _____
  _____
  _____
  _____
  _____
  _____

- How can I encourage or rebuke others through what I have learned? _____
  _____
  _____
  _____
  _____
  _____

- How is grace shown through this story? _____
  _____
  _____

_____
_____
_____
_____

• In what way is the gospel revealed through this situation?

_____
_____
_____
_____
_____
_____

6. Read Acts 10. Cornelius' family is only mentioned in passing but consider how his wife and children responded and what troubles they may have faced in the Roman culture because of their faith.

• Who are the main characters? _____

_____
_____
_____

• What other characters may be "unseen"? (Think of family members of these characters and how you would respond if you were transported back into history into this situation.)

_____
_____
_____
_____

• Which character traits are exemplary and should be used as a pattern for contemporary Christian living? _____

_____
_____
_____
_____

- Which character traits are unchristian and should be avoided or purged from a Christian's life? _____
  _____
  _____
  _____
  _____
  _____

- What is the crisis (or crises) faced? _____
  _____
  _____
  _____

- What is the proper Biblical response in this situation? _____
  _____
  _____
  _____
  _____
  _____
  _____

- How can I apply this to my life if I am faced with a similar situation?
  _____
  _____
  _____
  _____
  _____

- How can I encourage or rebuke others through what I have learned? _____
  _____
  _____
  _____
  _____
  _____

- How is grace shown through this story? _____

  _____

  _____

  _____

  _____

  _____

  _____

- In what way is the gospel revealed through this situation?

  _____

  _____

  _____

  _____

  _____

  _____

7. Read Acts 16:16-40. Think of what the Philippian jailor's wife must have thought when her husband walked into the house with two prisoners.

- Who are the main characters? _____

  _____

  _____

  _____

- What other characters may be "unseen"? (Think of family members of these characters and how you would respond if you were transported back into history into this situation.)

  _____

  _____

  _____

  _____

- Which character traits are exemplary and should be used as a pattern for contemporary Christian living? _____

  _____

  _____

_____
_____
_____
_____

- Which character traits are unchristian and should be avoided or purged from a Christian's life? _____
_____
_____
_____
_____
_____

- What is the crisis (or crises) faced? _____
_____
_____
_____

- What is the proper Biblical response in this situation?
_____
_____
_____
_____
_____
_____

- How can I apply this to my life if I am faced with a similar situation?
_____
_____
_____
_____
_____
_____

- How can I encourage or rebuke others through what I have learned? _____
_____

_____
_____
_____
_____
_____
_____

- How is grace shown through this story? _____
_____
_____
_____
_____
_____

- In what way is the gospel revealed through this situation?
_____
_____
_____
_____
_____

8. Read Acts 27-28:16. We read here about another Centurion who accompanied Paul to Rome. Look at his gradual transformation and imagine what it must have been like for his wife when he walked through the door and told her this story!

- Who are the main characters? _____
_____
_____

- What other characters may be "unseen"? (Think of family members of these characters and how you would respond if you were transported back into history into this situation.)
_____

_____
_____
_____

- Which character traits are exemplary and should be used as a pattern for contemporary Christian living? _____
_____
_____
_____
_____
_____

- Which character traits are unchristian and should be avoided or purged from a Christian's life? _____
_____
_____
_____
_____
_____

- What is the crisis (or crises) faced? _____
_____
_____
_____

- What is the proper Biblical response in this situation?
_____
_____
_____
_____
_____
_____

- How can I apply this to my life if I am faced with a similar situation? _____
_____
_____

_____

_____

_____

_____

- How can I encourage or rebuke others through what I have learned? _____

  _____

  _____

  _____

  _____

  _____

- How is grace shown through this story? _____

  _____

  _____

  _____

  _____

  _____

- In what way is the gospel revealed through this situation?

  _____

  _____

  _____

  _____

  _____

9. Read Ephesians 6:11-20; 2 Timothy 2:1-4; Philemon 1:1-2 and contemplate how we are to live as soldiers of the cross of Christ.

- Who are the main characters? _____

  _____

  _____

  _____

- What other characters may be "unseen"? (Think of family members of these characters and how you would respond if you were transported back into history into this situation.)

  _____
  _____
  _____
  _____

- Which character traits are exemplary and should be used as a pattern for contemporary Christian living? _____

  _____
  _____
  _____
  _____
  _____

- Which character traits are unchristian and should be avoided or purged from a Christian's life? _____

  _____
  _____
  _____
  _____
  _____

- What is the crisis (or crises) faced? _____

  _____
  _____
  _____

- What is the proper Biblical response in this situation?

  _____
  _____
  _____
  _____
  _____

- Howcan I apply this to my life if I am faced with a similar situation?

  _____

  _____

  _____

  _____

- How can I encourage or rebuke others through what I have learned? _____

  _____

  _____

  _____

  _____

  _____

- How is grace shown through this story? _____

  _____

  _____

  _____

  _____

  _____

- In what way is the gospel revealed through this situation?

  _____

  _____

  _____

  _____

  _____

10. The greatest Commander is the Lord Jesus Christ; He provides the perfect example in Scripture for us as Christians. Read Joshua 5:13-15 and Revelation 19:11-20. Joshua 5:13-15 tells how Christ (pre-incarnate) revealed himself to Joshua as his Commander. Revelation

19:11-20 shows that Christ Himself will lead the final battle as the ultimate commander: King of Kings and Lord of Lords.

- Who is the main character? _____
  _____
  _____
  _____

- What other characters may be "unseen"? (Think of family members of these characters and how you would respond if you were transported back into history into this situation.)
  _____
  _____
  _____
  _____

- Which character traits are exemplary and should be used as a pattern for contemporary Christian living? _____
  _____
  _____
  _____
  _____
  _____

- Which character traits are unchristian and should be avoided or purged from a Christian's life? _____
  _____
  _____
  _____
  _____
  _____

- What is the crisis (or crises) faced? _____
  _____
  _____
  _____

- What is the proper Biblical response in this situation?

  _____

  _____

  _____

  _____

  _____

  _____

- HowcanIapplythistomylifeifIamfacedwithasimilarsituation?

  _____

  _____

  _____

  _____

  _____

- How can I encourage or rebuke others through what I have learned? _____

  _____

  _____

  _____

  _____

  _____

  _____

- How is grace shown through this story? _____

  _____

  _____

  _____

  _____

- In what way is the gospel revealed through this situation?

  _____

  _____

  _____

  _____

  _____

Final Thoughts

You are never alone. I hope that as you have read through this devotional book you can say with certainty that others in a military setting have gone before you and kept the faith. Like us, they failed and sinned many times, but the promise of Romans 8:37 remains as true today as when it was first penned, that in "all these things we [can be] more than conquerors through him that loved us."

My husband recently returned home from a one year deployment to Afghanistan. The experiences I faced were among the hardest and most stressful God has allowed me to go through up. We've been through a lot of trying times as a couple, yet every separation we endured was different and our military support system changed somewhat with each one. However, from my personal experience I can confidently say that God alone is the *one* Person you can depend on *always*. He can and will help you in ways that no human can. His Spirit provides comfort when you are sad or grieving. He provides grace when you don't feel like you can extend a kind word to one more individual. He gives hope and strength when you are physically drained and don't think you can possibly take one more step. His mercy uplifts you and His loving-kindness brings both motivation and joy through each day. Think about it, the *sovereign Creator of the universe* cared enough for *you* to send his only Son for *your* sins. John 3:16 says clearly, "For God so loved the world, that he gave his only begotten Son, that whosoever believeth in him should not perish, but have everlasting life." If you have never trusted Christ as your personal Savior, I implore you to look at the following passages in Scripture and make the decision to receive Christ today. You and I are both sinners and deserve death as the penalty for our sin. Yet, God in His love sent Jesus to die on the cross as our personal substitute so that His wrath might be avenged. This free gift can be yours if you confess your sin to God and call upon Him in faith. Doing good works will never be enough to pay for the penalty of sin. It requires faith, believing that Christ's sacrifice is sufficient for your eternal salvation.

Romans 3:23- "For all have sinned, and come short of the glory of God;"

Romans 6:23- "For the wages of sin *is* death; but the gift of God *is* eternal life through Jesus Christ our Lord."

Hebrews 9:27- "And as it is appointed unto men once to die, but after this the judgment:"

Romans 5:8- "But God commendeth his love toward us, in that, while we were yet sinners, Christ died for us."

Ephesians 2:8-9- "For by grace are ye saved through faith; and that not of yourselves: *it is* the gift of God: Not of works, lest any man should boast."

Romans 10:13- "For whosoever shall call upon the name of the Lord shall be saved."

Lastly, one of the important realities I hope to convey to you is the Holy Spirit's amazing ability to guide you into all truth. As Christ in John 16:13 states, "Howbeit when he, the Spirit of truth, is come, he will guide you into all truth: for he shall not speak of himself; but whatsoever he shall hear, *that* shall he speak: and he will show you things to come." The Christian life is a walk of faith as we obey Scripture with the Spirit's guiding (Romans 15:4). In fact, it is the power of God in us that works us "to will and to do of His good pleasure" (Philippians 2:13). Despite all our failures, God will complete the good work He has begun in us (Philippians 1:6) by His grace. To Him be the glory!

The Johnson family the day Chaplain Johnson returned
home from his yearlong deployment to Afghanistan.

LaVergne, TN USA
08 September 2010
196385LV00004B/2/P